10 Things to prep for S.H.T.F

By:
Edna Stowell

This book is for all the people that want to be prepared for anything this crazy world can bring to their door.

This is a book of the top ten things I think you should prep for a S.H.T.F event. You may have other things on your list but everyone's list will be a little different. This is because prepping for S.H.T.F can be very personnel. There are some things we all need to live but there are other things that are just for you or your family.

Number 1

Food:

This is the first thing most people put on their list because it is very important. This is also a prep that can be done very cheaply or you can spend a lot of money on it. There are a few things that you have to make sure you take into account when buying this prep:

1) Salt- to much salt in a food could help to dehydrate you in a time that water may be scares.

2) protein- Your body needs protein to help build a better body.

3) how it is made- You need to

be able to make this food on the move. So you don't want it to be very complicated.

4) Size and weight- You may have to be carrying three days or more of food along with other things. If it is to heavy it may making hiking to your bug out location very difficult.

5) Calories: You are going to be burning more calories then normal. So higher calorie food will help. I know this goes against everything we are told on T.V. today remember your body will need this to help you to keep moving.

There are many different places we can buy food to prep. If you are prepping on a budget the dollar store and Wal-Mart are good place to start. Some areas also have scratch and dent stores were you can get canned for cheaper. There are some places online that you can get cheap freeze dried foods or soups. If you have no budget then you can just pick up extra food every time you go shopping for you family. OR Some online place have a monthly plan were they send you food every month. Different things so it will be harder to make sure you get things you eat.

You have to make sure you know what is in the food that you buy if you have any food allergies. Another thing you have to watch is food expiration dates. Some foods you can get have long shelf life others not so long. So you should check them before you buy them.

Food for your bug out location:

When buying food for your bug out location is a little easier then buying them for your bug out bag. You still have to watch salt, calories, and how it is made but hopeful you have storied your food there long before you needed it.

Some good Bug out location foods would be:

Cereal
Bisques/flour
Sugar
Freeze dried milk
Juice mix
Marshmallows
Peanut butter
Rice
Beans
Corn
Caned /dehydrated stew
Soups

Dehydrated meats
Tuna fish
Jams/jellies

Anything that can be made shelf stable by dehydrating or canning would be great for this location. It would also be a great thing for you to learn how to can and dehydrate foods. Some community centers offer classes in these areas.

BELOW I AM LEAVING SPACE FOR
YOU TO WRITE ANYTHING YOU
WOULD LIKE TO THIS SECTION

Number 2

Water:

This is the most important prep to have for both bugging out/ bug out location and bugging in. So we will look at each way.

Bugging out:

You can only carry so much water with you in your bug out bag. So it is good to have a life straw or some way to filter water you may find on your way . You could also boil water to help make it safer for you to drink.

Bug out location:

At your bug out location it would be good to have a way to collect rain water. It would also be good to have a stream, lake or river near by that you can get water from for drinking, watering crops, cleaning clothes and bathing.

You can also have cases of water that you put at this location before you S.H.T.F. This water would be good for brushing teeth and drinking.

Bugging in:

This is much like bug out location hopefully you have prepared before you needed it. But you could also buy a bag called a BoB. This goes into your bathtub and can hold up to 62 gallons of water. This water would be good to use for personal hygiene and flashing toilets.

Again knowing of a close by water source would be good information just in case you need it. You should still have away to boil or clean the water before drinking it.

BELOW I AM LEAVING SPACE FOR

YOU TO WRITE ANYTHING YOU
WOULD LIKE TO THIS SECTION

Number 3

Clothes

Clothes are little harder to prep because you could change sizes due to many different factors. So going to your local thrift store to buy clothes would be a good idea so you can get different sizes at a small price to your wallets. This would also be good if you have children because they are going to keep growing .

You can also shop the clearance sales or going out of business sales for clothes at a discount price..

BELOW I AM LEAVING SPACE FOR

YOU TO WRITE ANYTHING YOU
WOULD LIKE TO THIS SECTION

Number 4

Medications:

This again is a personal need area of prepping. But it is always good to have some basic medication on hand just in case. Most of these medication can be bought at a minimal prices at many different stores. But if you know you need a name brand medication then you can try to find them on clearance or found coupons for these medication.

Examples of the medication you may want to have with you would be:
Pain killer
Anti- diarrhea

Multi vitamin
Cold/flu
Allergy
Bandages
Cough drops
Cough
Antibiotics
Items to clean wounds

BELOW I AM LEAVING SPACE FOR
YOU TO WRITE ANYTHING YOU
WOULD LIKE TO THIS SECTION

Number 5

Shoes:

Just like clothes you will want to buy different sizes if you have children so they can have the new size they need as they grow. It would also be good to have at least three pairs for each adult you have in your group.

You may also want to have different types of shoes to do different things. For example:

1) sneakers- these would be good for working around the bug out location or to have on in your bug in location in case you have to leave but can

return went it is safe again.

2) work boots-to wear when you have to fix things around your area and need extra protection on your feet

3)hiking boots- these are best if you have to walk long distance over uneven ground. It would help you not to twist your ankle.

BELOW I AM LEAVING SPACE FOR
YOU TO WRITE ANYTHING YOU
WOULD LIKE TO THIS SECTION

Number 6

Shelter:

Bugging In:

If you are bugging in you already have shelter but you may want to have things to put over the windows to keep people from seeing in and getting the layout of your location.

Bugging out:

Tents, trailers, or a camper are all useful for this event. The tent would be good if you are having to walk out or could not use a vehicle. But make sure you have all you need to go with the tent like sleeping bags, sleeping pads, pillows, rope, stacks, and traps.

Trailers and campers are good to have if you can use a vehicle to bug out.. This is also good because you can have it prepacked and may be able to leave faster. But with these you may want to have some kind of cameo trap or netting to help hide it when you are sleeping.

BELOW I AM LEAVING SPACE FOR
YOU TO WRITE ANYTHING YOU
WOULD LIKE TO THIS SECTION

Number 7

Weapon:

These is something that is complete up to you and your family/group. But it would most likely be in you good interest to have at least a knife on you to help you with fishing and trapping food if you need to do such things.

If you want it may also be good to have a hand gun along with a hunting rifle. These can be used for both hinting and protection of your family/ group. To go with these weapons you would want to have at least 2000 extra rounds of ammo. Again you can shop around to get the best prices on the ammo. You will also want to get training on both guns that you will have to use.

BELOW I AM LEAVING SPACE FOR
YOU TO WRITE ANYTHING YOU
WOULD LIKE TO THIS SECTION

Number 8

Fire starter:

Having a way to start fires for heat, cooking and light will be very useful. Lighters, matches, windproof matches, and waterproof match are all good things to have for this area.

But you may also want to have fire starter or timber to start fires with you. Just in case you can 't find anything to start the fire with in your area.

BELOW I AM LEAVING SPACE FOR
YOU TO WRITE ANYTHING YOU
WOULD LIKE TO THIS SECTION

Number 9

Hygiene kit:

This is also an area that is personnel to each prepper. But it would be a good idea to have some basic items such as:

Toothpaste
Toothbrush
Soap
Shampoo
Deodorant
Hairbrush
comb
Hair ties

Keeping up with these basic things may help the change of environment and keeping people out of shock due to all the changes they will have to make.

BELOW I AM LEAVING SPACE FOR
YOU TO WRITE ANYTHING YOU
WOULD LIKE TO THIS SECTION

Number 10

Something to help with the change:

This is an area that most prepper would say that there are more important thing to have but as a parent I think having thing that will make the change easier on my children will make thing easier on me and my family/group. These would be things like favorite blankets/ pillows, coloring books, crayons/ colored pencils, stuffed animals, or anything that may relate to your children or yourself.

BELOW I AM LEAVING SPACE FOR

YOU TO WRITE ANYTHING YOU
WOULD LIKE TO THIS SECTION

These is an area for you to write your bug out / bug in plans. It is sometimes easier for you to make plan after read this type of book but it can be hard to go back and forth between the book you read and a note pad. So I am putting it area here in the book to make it easier for you.

Bug in plan:

Bug out Plan:

Location:

Number of people: